THIS COLORING BOOK BELOGNS TO :

thing that start with letter A ?

APPLE

thing that start with letter B?

BIRD

thing that start with letter C ?

COW

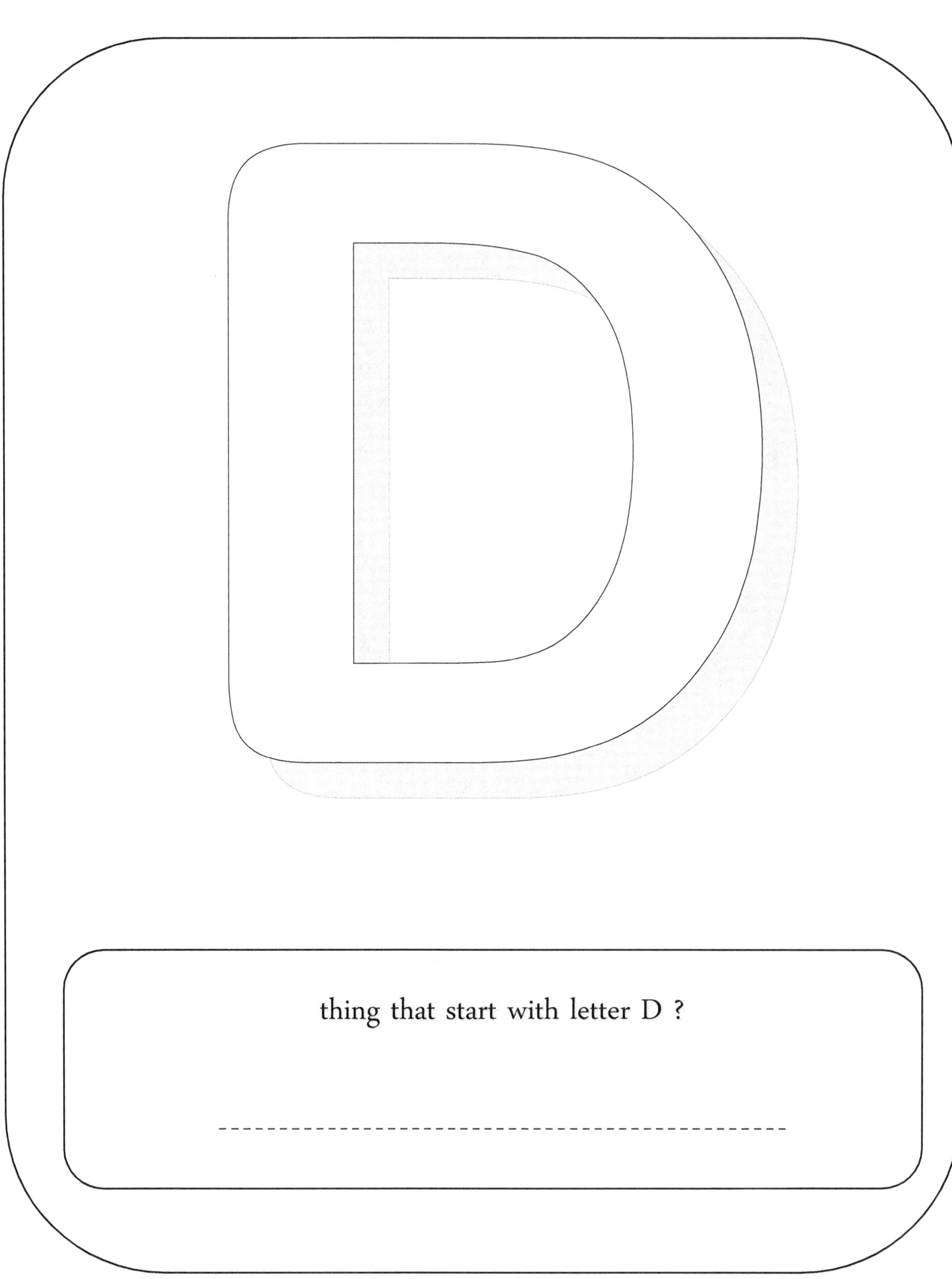

thing that start with letter D ?

DUCk

thing that start with letter E ?

____

ELEPHANT

thing that start with letter F ?

FISH

thing that start with letter G ?

GIFT

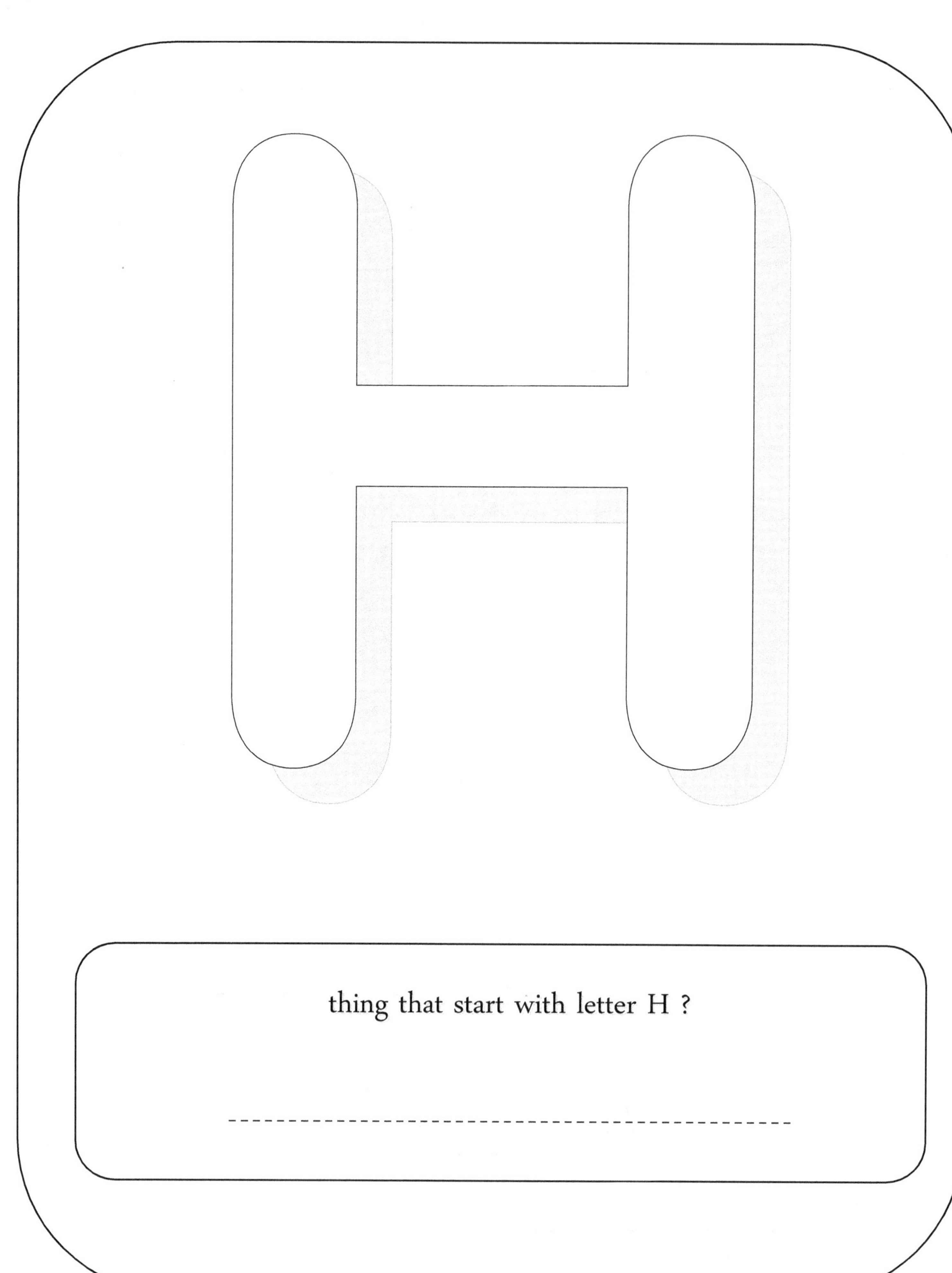
thing that start with letter H ?

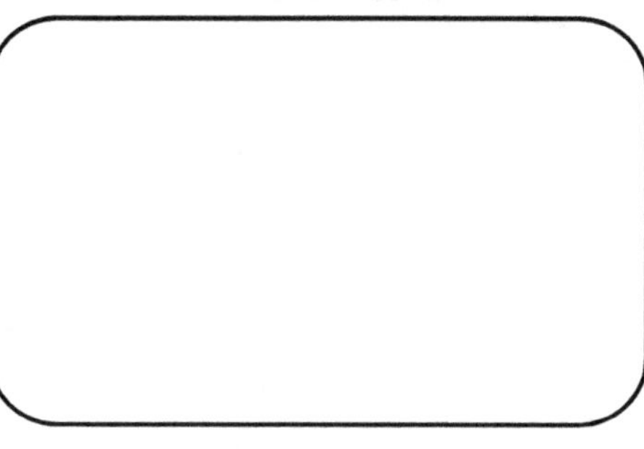

HOUSE

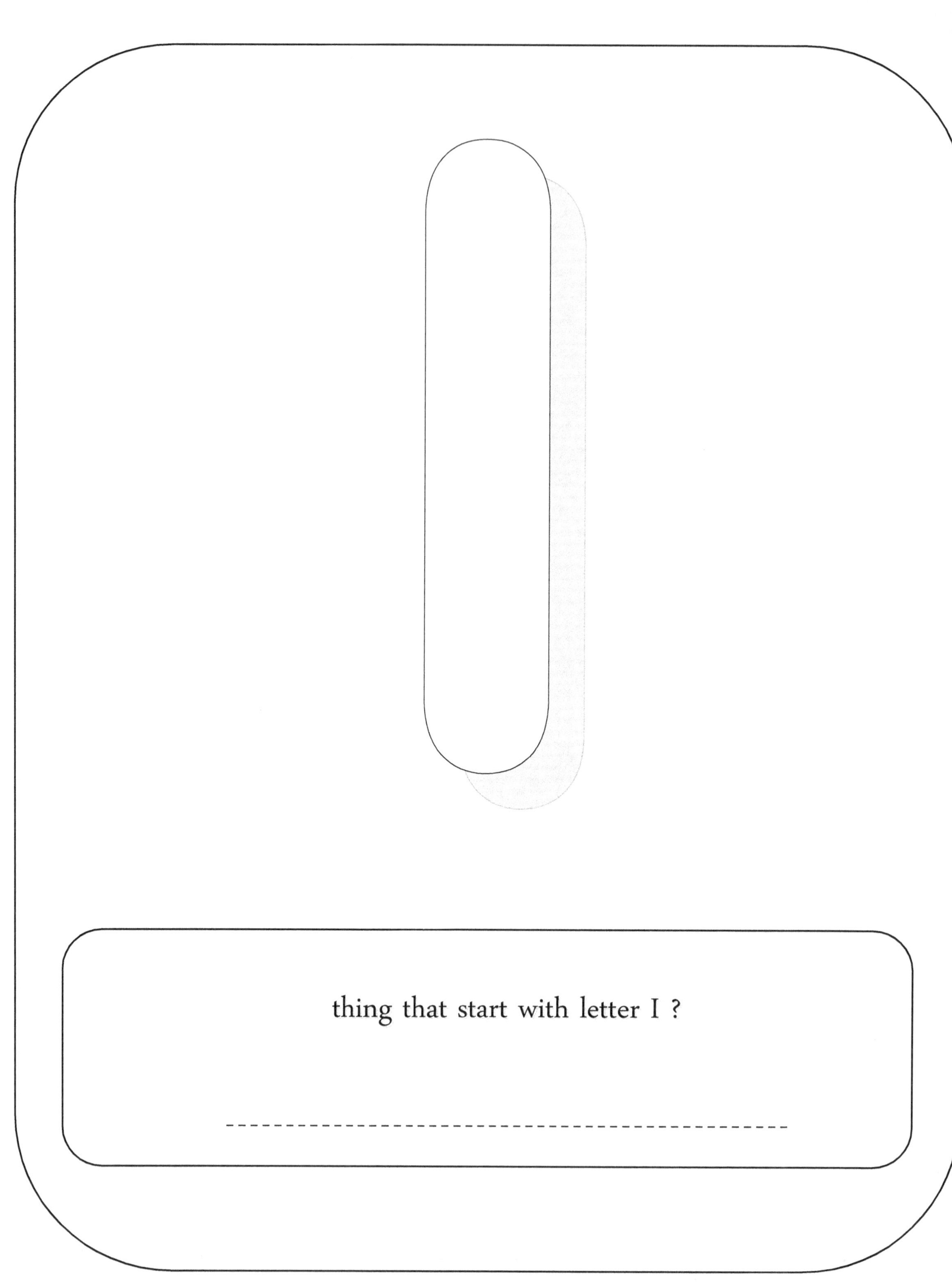

thing that start with letter I ?

ICE cream

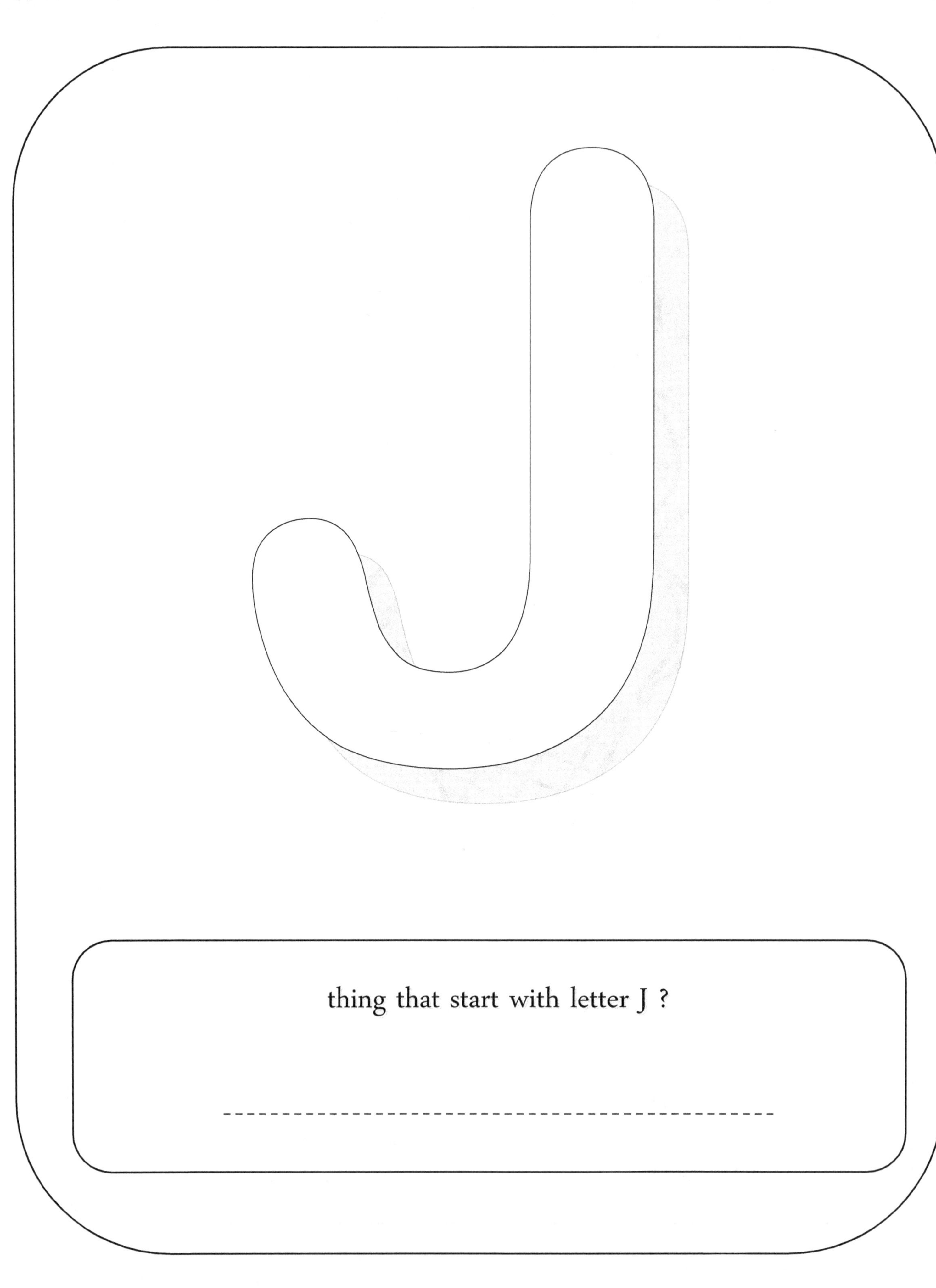

thing that start with letter J ?

JUG

thing that start with letter K ?

KIDS

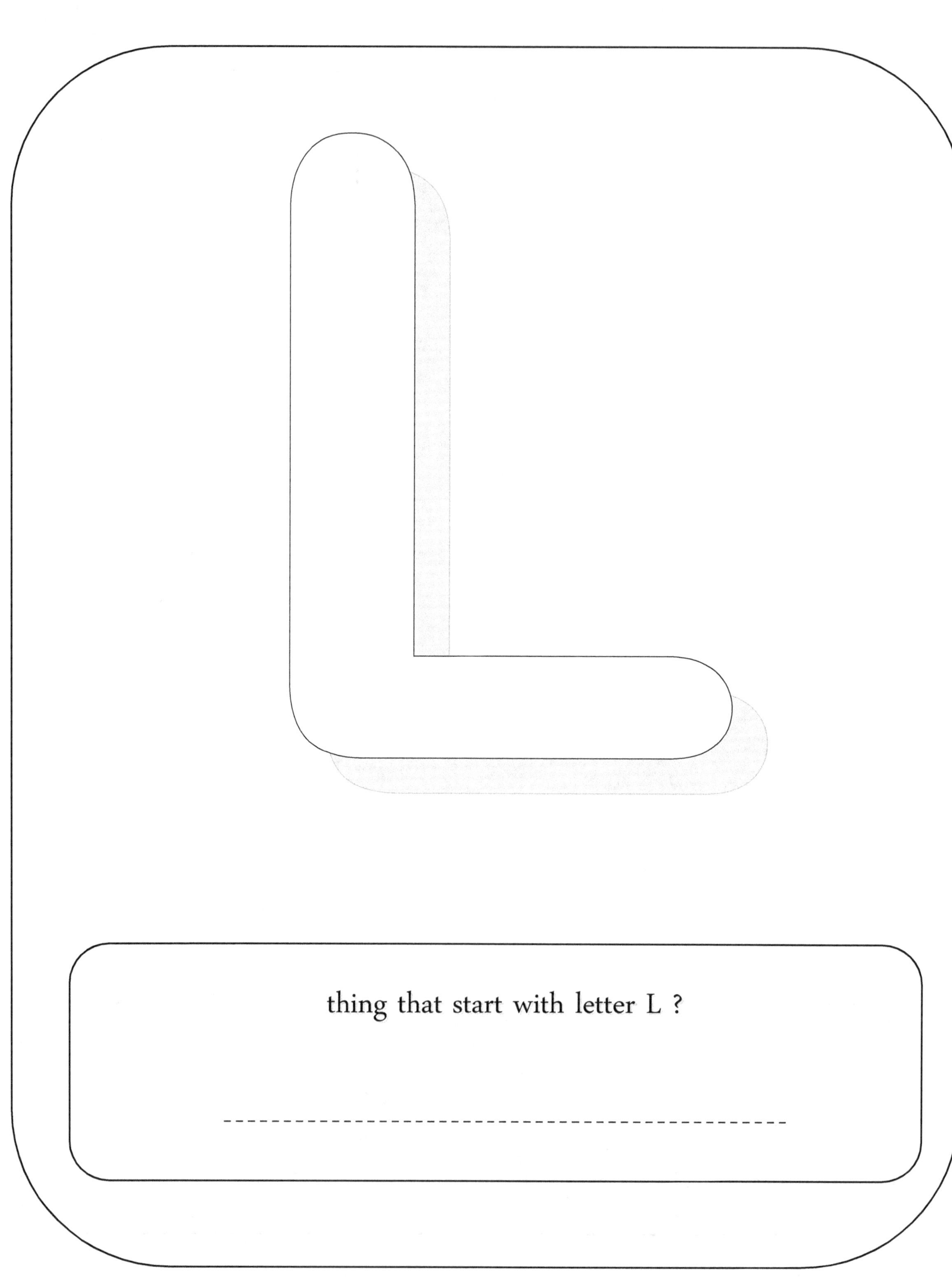
thing that start with letter L ?

LION

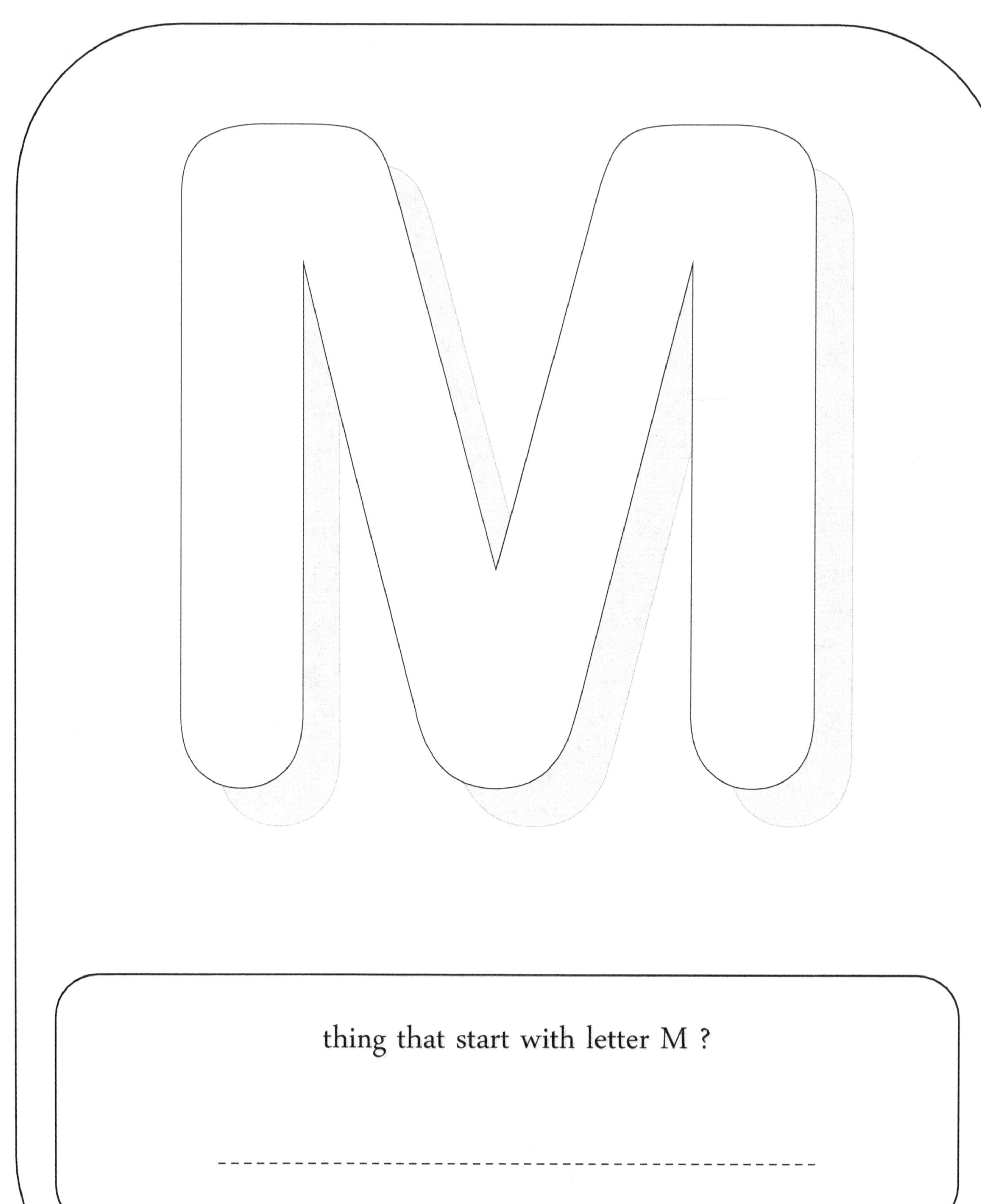

thing that start with letter M ?

MERAID

thing that start with letter N ?

NEST

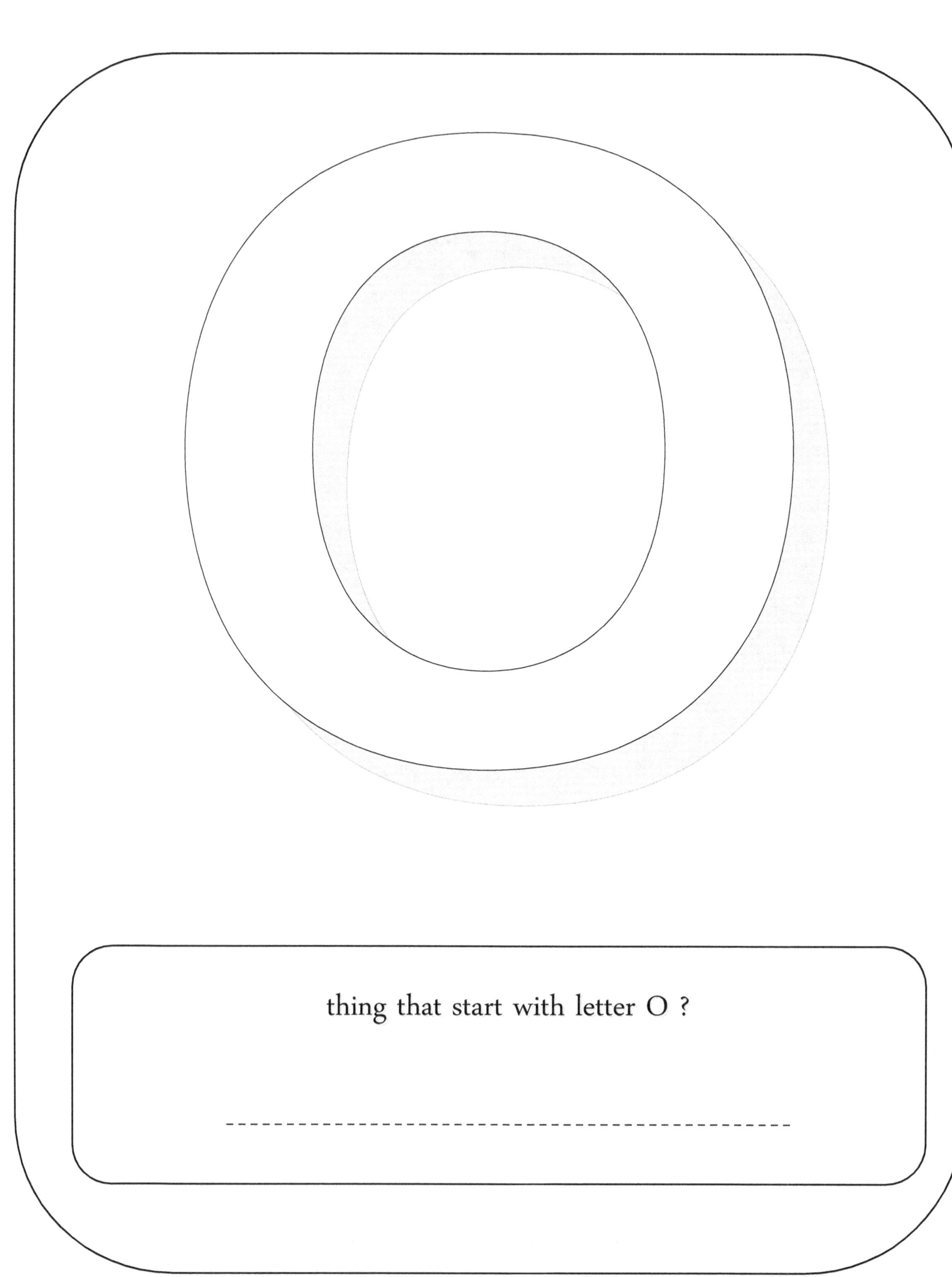

thing that start with letter O ?

ORANGE

thing that start with letter P ?

PANDA

thing that start with letter Q ?

QUESTION

thing that start with letter R ?

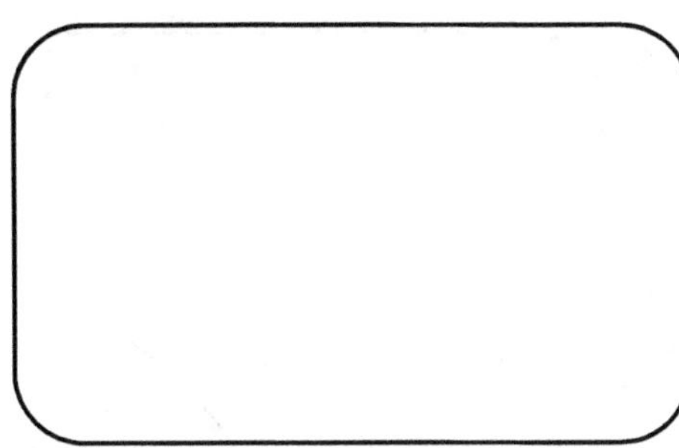

RABBIT

thing that start with letter S ?

SUN

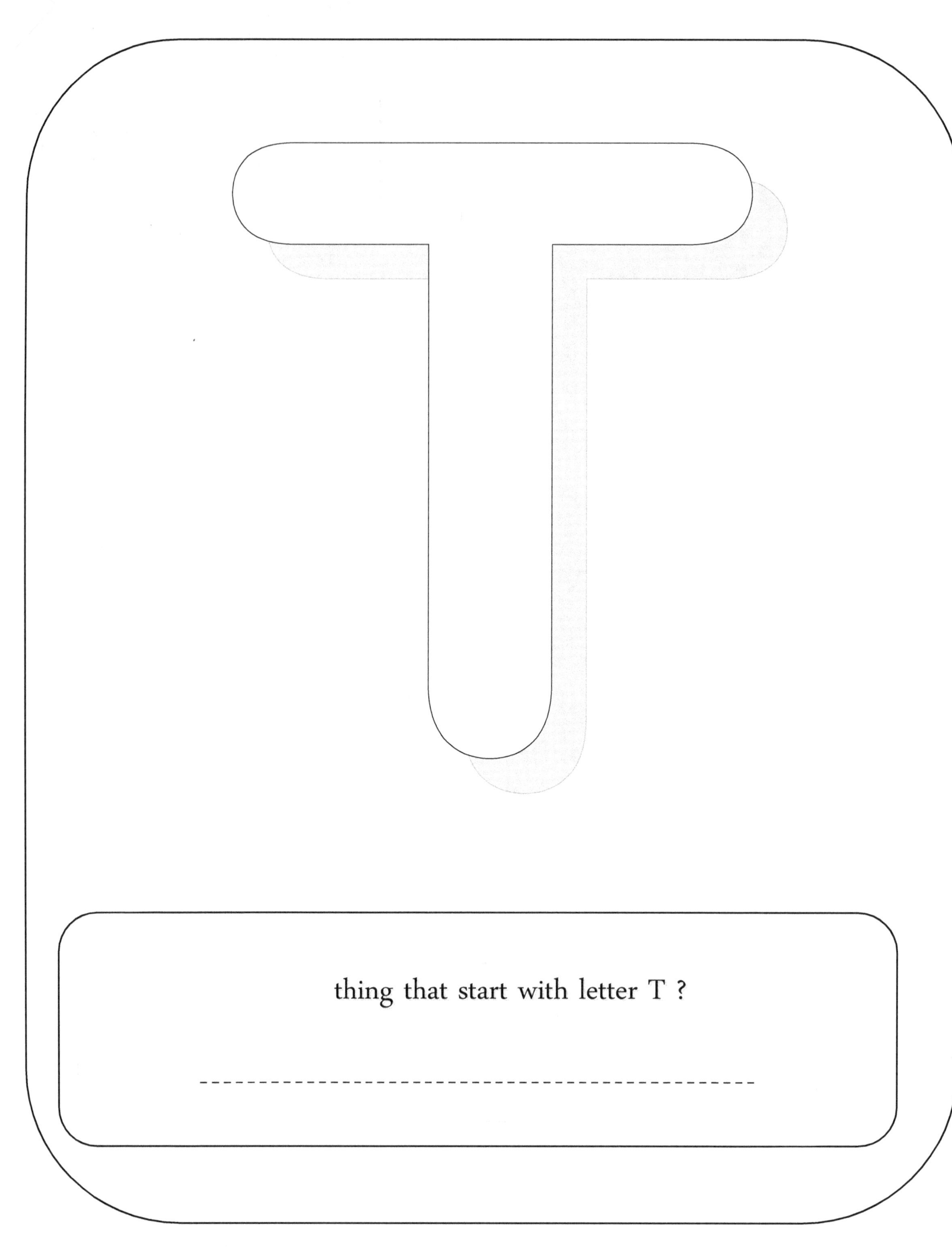
thing that start with letter T ?

TABLE

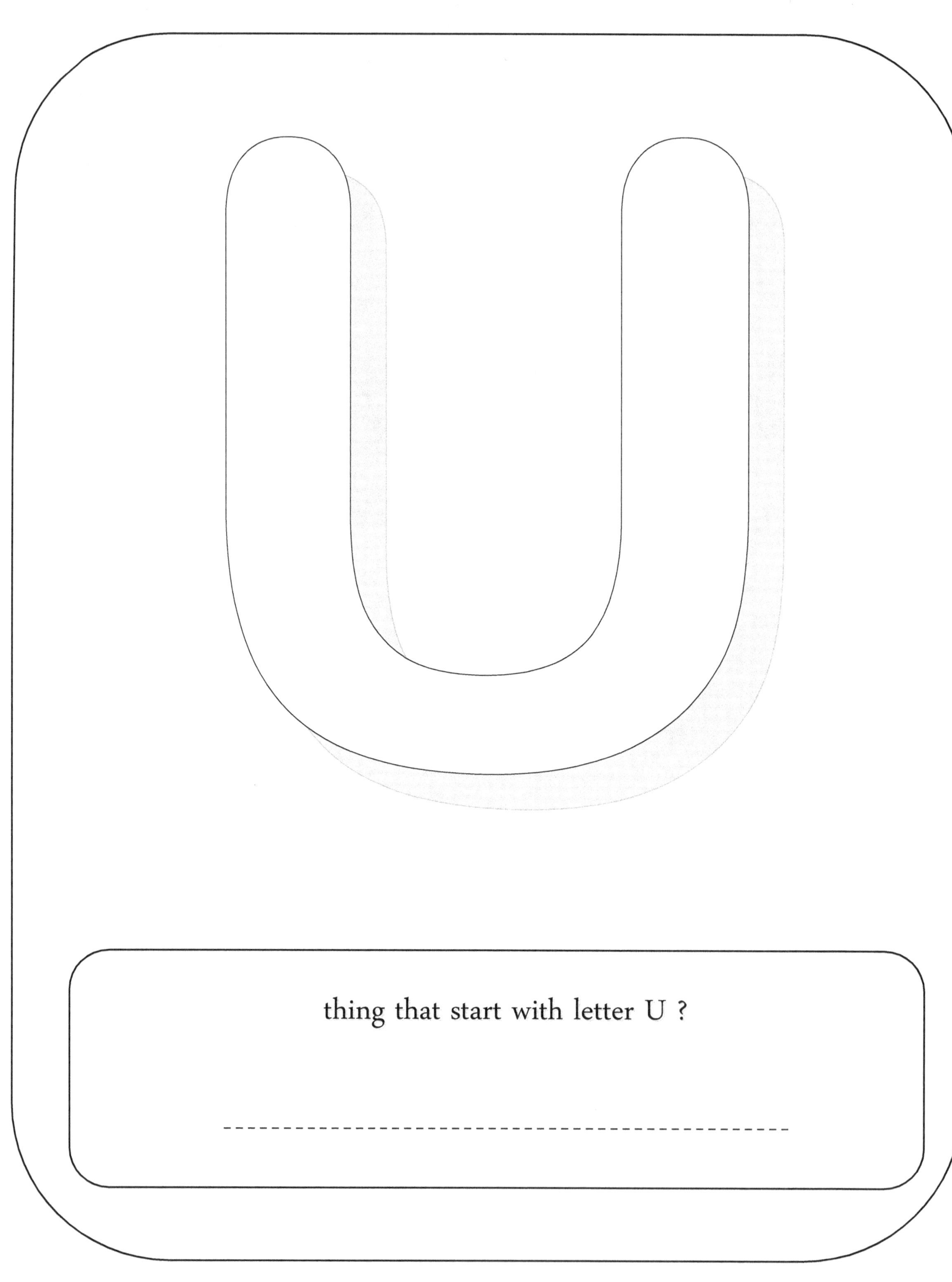
thing that start with letter U ?

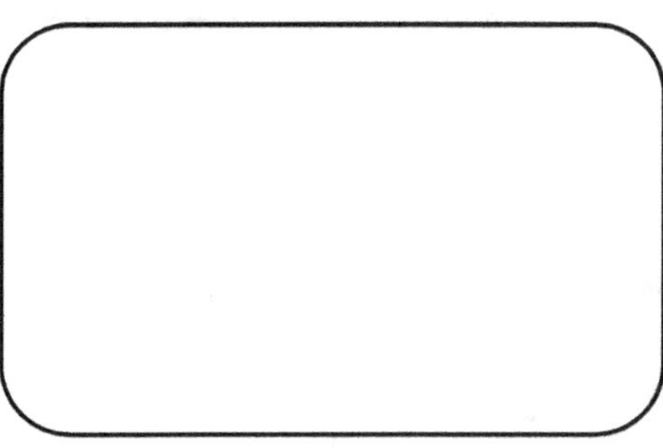

UBRELLA

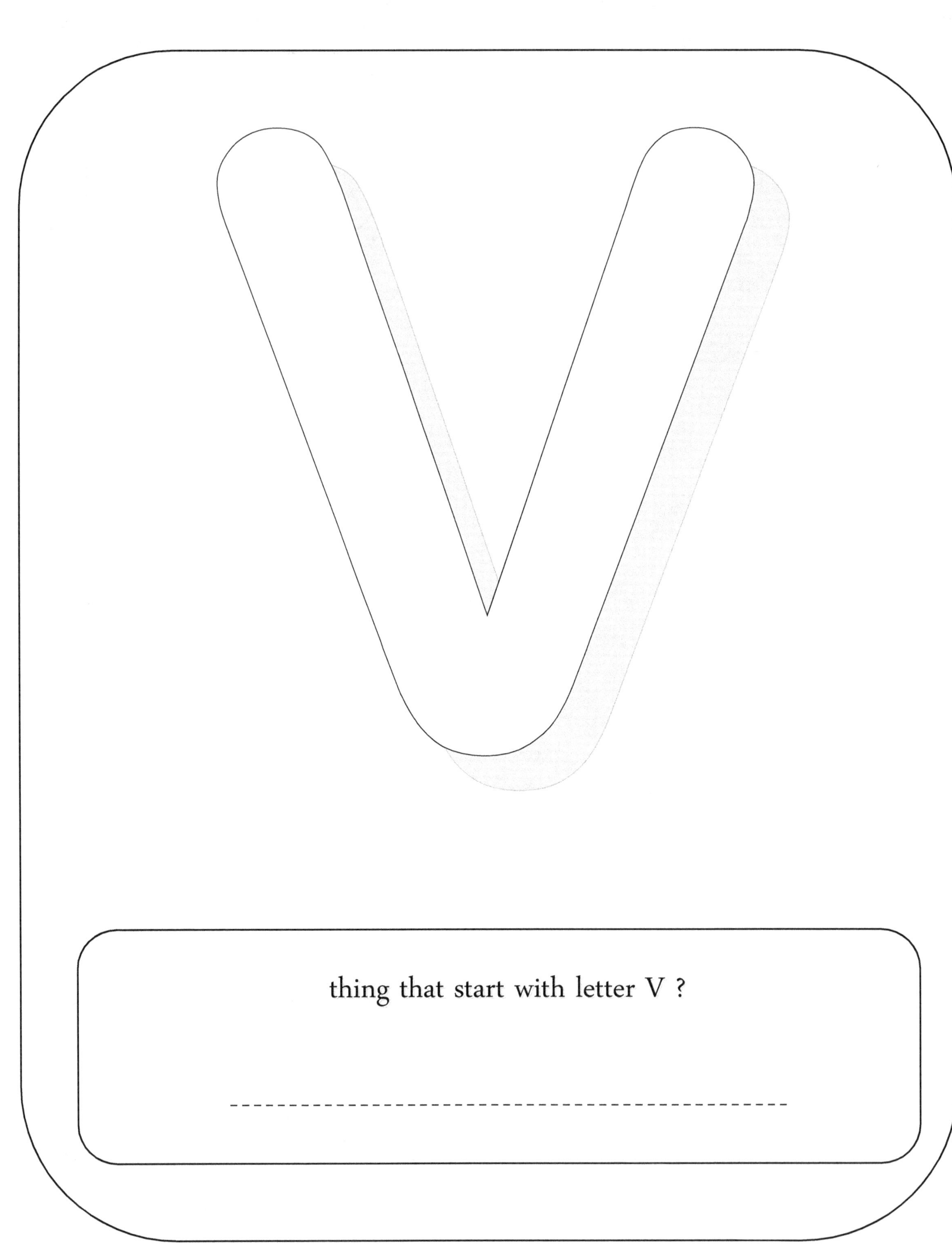

thing that start with letter V ?

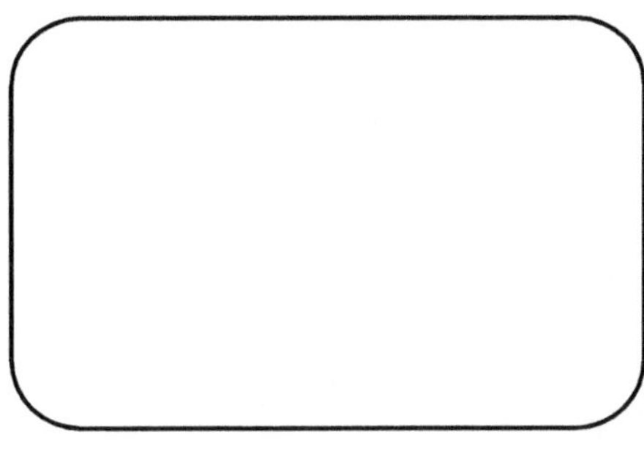

vegetables

thing that start with letter w ?

WARLUS

thing that start with letter X ?

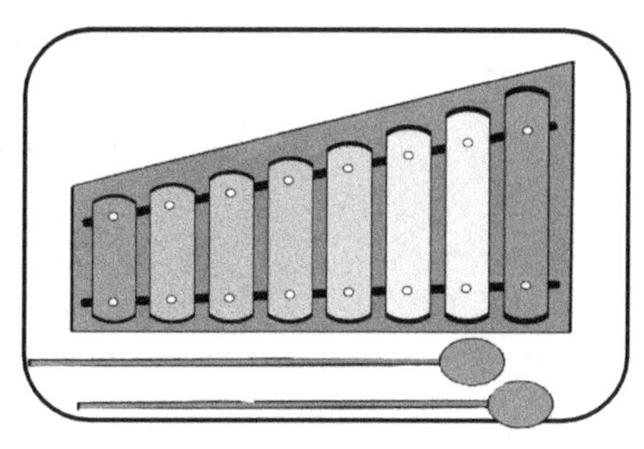

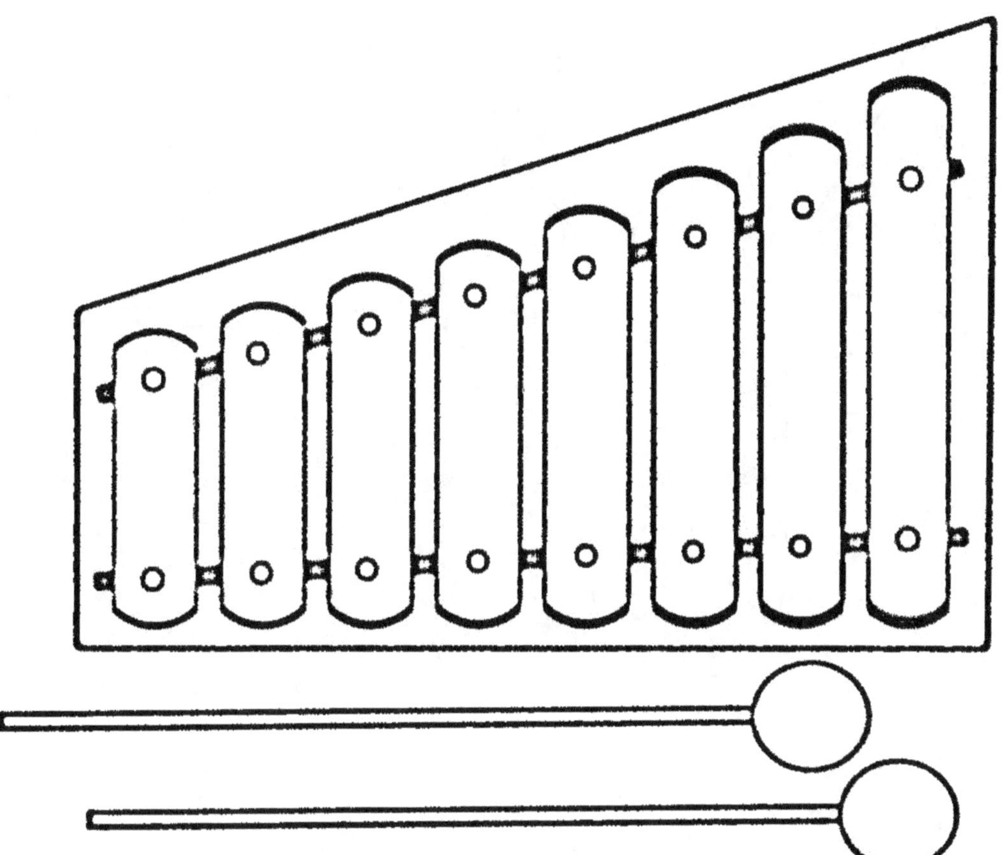

XYLOPHONE

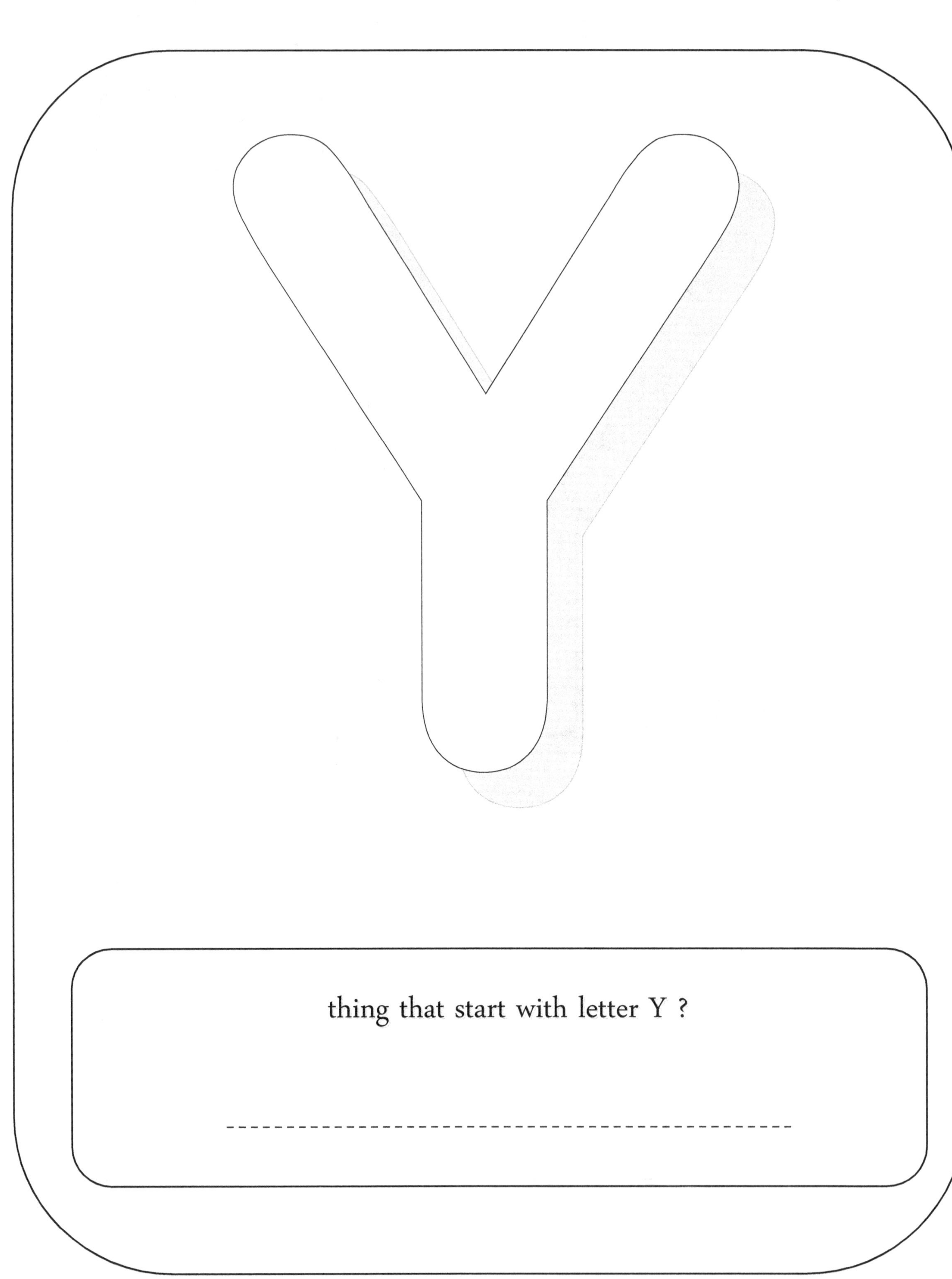
thing that start with letter Y ?

YAK

thing that start with letter Z ?

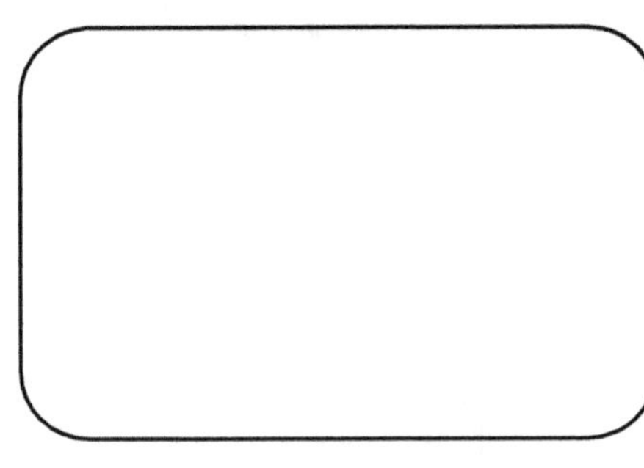

ZEBRA

www.ingramcontent.com/pod-product-compliance
Lightning Source LLC
Chambersburg PA
CBHW081457250726
48662CB00009B/3120